BL484 x2

PEACE MOVES

D1477748

PEACE MOVES NUCLEAR PROTEST IN THE 1980s

Photographs by Ed Barber

Text by Zoë Fairbairns and James Cameron

Chatto & Windus · The Hogarth Press   London

Published in 1984 by
Chatto & Windus · The Hogarth Press
40 William IV Street,
London WC2N 4DF

All rights reserved. No part of this publication may be
reproduced, stored in a retrieval system, or transmitted in any
form, or by any means, electronic, mechanical, photocopying,
recording or otherwise, without the prior permission of the
publisher.

British Library Cataloguing in Publication Data
Barber, Ed
    Peace moves.
    1. Peace—Societies, etc
    2. Great Britain—Politics and government
    I. Title   II. Fairbairns, Zoë
    III. Cameron, James
    327.1'72'0941   JX1908.G7
    ISBN 0-7011-2828-3

Photographs and Author's note copyright © Ed Barber 1984
Foreword copyright © James Cameron 1984
'Taking it personally' copyright © Zoë Fairbairns 1984

Printed in Great Britain by
Butler & Tanner Ltd
Frome, Somerset

CONTENTS

To my Mum and Dad

Author's note

Photographers have been documenting war for nearly a century, doubtless attracted as much by the glamour and adventure as by a genuine concern for humanity and suffering. Peace campaigns have not drawn such sustained photographic attention, unless the mainstream media deem 'peace' to be newsworthy. Then the cameras and film crews arrive en masse. As the Falklands conflict ably demonstrated, war is good for business. It certainly sells newspapers – every day there are reports of wars all over the world.

Our society has been conditioned to accept war as an inevitable spectacle that takes place somewhere else. But nuclear war would take place closer to home. Britain is fast becoming an aircraft-carrier loaded with nuclear weaponry, making us a prime target in any nuclear conflict. People's resistance to the nuclear threat is growing, yet the Peace Movement is almost invisible.

This book is an attempt to put on record the peace demonstrations and actions of the last four years – to make the Peace Movement part of a visible history. I see this as preventative photography. The photographs here are both a celebration and a warning. They run counter to the prevailing flow of images in our culture, where war is normalised and made palatable.

I would like to thank the many organisations and individuals who have helped and supported my work – in particular Peter Brawne, Alice Cook, Mike Goldwater, Helen John, Lorie Karlin, Peter Kennard, Gwyn Kirk, Deborah Law, Jenny Matthews, Paul Trevor and Belinda Whiting for their advice and encouragement.

1 [overleaf] Hyde Park, October 1981

Forword James Cameron

When the Campaign for Nuclear Disarmament came into being in 1958, and gave its initials to the most specialised yet universal expression of human reason in a world that seemed to be going quite perceptibly insane, Ed Barber was just nine years old.

That was almost a quarter-century ago, so Ed Barber has been lucky. So have we. And luck is a very unreliable thing to trust when the stake is human survival. Ed Barber knows that; I know it; the people who are the subject of this book know it. More and more become aware of it every day. Where the new-born CND counted its activists in their hundreds, almost all in our own vulnerable country, they are now counted in their hundreds of thousands, and virtually all over the world.

That is still not enough. That is why the Greenham Common women have been at their uncomfortable and lonely vigil for so long. That is why Ed Barber's camera recorded for us their endurance, and their courage. They, and we, are fortunate in that the Greenham phenomenon attracted the sympathy and skill of a great photographer.

To say that the anti-nuclear movement began modestly would itself be pretty modest. To be sure it was small, and dismissed, as every British expression of idealism is dismissed, as 'eccentric'. But it was an articulate infant from its birthday; its function was to wake up the neighbours, wake up the country, if possible wake up the world. The world took some waking up, but there are strong signs that this is happening at last. If so, 'Greenham' may become as symbolic a word today as 'Aldermaston' was in the Sixties.

I may be allowed a moment's reminiscence. In the days of CND's birth it meant as much to me as it means today to Ed, and the Greenham women, and after all these years it still does.

I was on the original founding committee which, with the exception of me, was composed of pretty distinguished men. I had been invited into this company of my betters for an almost accidental reason – among them all I was the only one, perhaps the only one in the country, who had seen atom-bombs in action. I had been the British observer at the atomic explosion tests at Bikini in the Pacific and Woomera in Australia. I had also, for my sins, seen the ruins of Hiroshima. The effect on me was indelible, and informs all my thinking to this day.

The protesters of today, the Greenham women and their colleagues everywhere, have not my easy personal and emotional excuse. Some are old enough to remember a cosy old pre-atomic world, but most, as you can see, are not arguing from nostalgia; they are young and vigorous and sanguine; they were not even born when Hiroshima and Nagasaki punctuated the world forever between hope and fear. They have lived with the atomic threat all their lives, yet they are nevertheless ready and indeed even eager to subject themselves to this sort of hardship, and sometimes even scorn, to persuade the world that suicide is a preposterous way of settling ideologies.

I am complimented to be able to introduce Ed Barber's book; I am far more grateful to him for having made it. He, and the Greenham women, and indeed I, must continue the old song we have been chanting these thirty years: 'We Shall Overcome - Some Day'.

The people and the protest

2 Westminster, June 1980

3 Trafalgar Square, October 1980

4 E. P. Thompson, Trafalgar Square, October 1980

5 Hyde Park, June 1980

6 Bruce Kent (General Secretary of CND) and Annajoy David (Youth CND), blockade of Royal Ordnance Factory, Burghfield, Berks, March 1983

7 Peace Chain, Atomic Weapons Research Establishment, Aldermaston, Berks, April 1983

8 Trafalgar Square, October 1980

9 Trafalgar Square, October 1980

10 Picket of Russian Embassy, London, June 1983

11 Hyde Park, October 1981

12 Hyde Park, June 1982

13 Hyde Park, October 1981

14 Hyde Park, October 1981

15 Spring Festival, USAF/RAF Greenham Common, Berks, March 1982

16 Hyde Park, October 1981

17 Visit of US Defence Secretary Casper Weinberger, Chatham House, London, October 1981

18 Hyde Park, October 1981

19 Leicester Square, September 1982

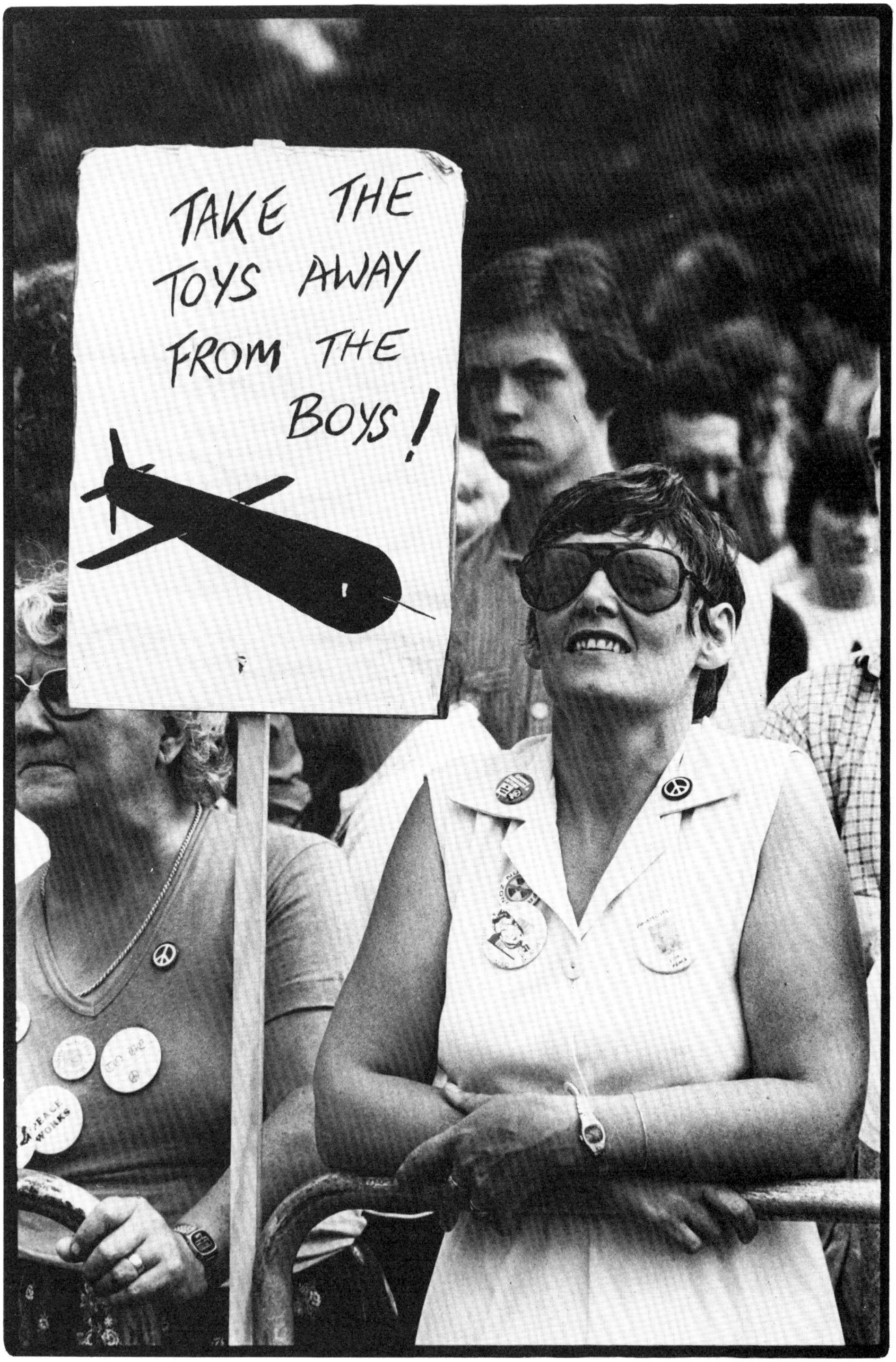
TAKE THE
TOYS AWAY
FROM THE
BOYS!

20 Hyde Park, June 1982

21 Veteran peace campaigner Lord Fenner Brockway's 93rd birthday celebration, Westminster, November 1981

22 Victoria Embankment, May 1983

23 Westminster, May 1983

24 Aldermaston, April 1983

25 Embrace the Base, Greenham Common, December 1982

26 Hyde Park, October 1981

27 Hyde Park, June 1982

Text on signs in image: "He shall bear their iniquities Isaiah 53:11" and "Greenham–Burghfield Good Friday 1983" and "..in the nuclear valley"

29 Padworth Common, Berks, April 1983   **30** [overleaf] Peace Chain, Aldermaston, April 1983. 70,000 people took part

Taking it personally Zoë Fairbairns

This book celebrates the peace movement in Britain in the early 1980s. It is an alternative to the countless other books you can buy which celebrate the war movement.

If you have never heard of the war movement, that is because it does not call itself that. Probably it does not even think of itself as a movement, it has no plans to move anywhere unless it is upwards and outwards and forwards, cloudlike, smokelike, cancerlike. Nor does it see itself as an alternative. It is normal. Its specialist books need no specialist bookstore, they're there at your station newsagent's: War Machines! The World's Most Comprehensive Encyclopedia of Military Weapons of the Twentieth Century! The Winds of War! Harrier! Action Adventure for the Death Dealing British Superjet! The Screaming Eagles, 101st Airborne! Kill or Die! Assault Troop! No 1 Blood Beach, No 2 Death in the Forest! Miniature Wargamer! The New Monthly Magazine for the Discerning War Gamer! Its films are on at your local Odeon; its donations are our income taxes; its news is mainstream national news; and when, in pursuit of its political ends, the war movement establishes settlements on common land, causing horror and disgust to other groups of human beings living nearby, it is not the war movement whose personnel are arrested, evicted, fined and jailed, even though they are openly conspiring to commit terrible crimes.

Sometimes the war movement says to the peace movement: not only are you dangerously naive with your pacifism, your unilateralism; not only that, but you are self-righteously unjust too. Don't you know we *all* hate war?

To which anyone who has participated in or seen the nonviolent life-loving imagery of peace movement demonstrations and compared that with the raucous bloodlust implicit in war movement demos (which needless to say are not called that) can only

reply, you could have fooled us.

If the war movement hated war, there would be no war.

And if that seems too naive a thought, move it down a notch or two: if the war movement hated war, there would be no *celebration* of war.

Successful soldiers would not march in triumph down the street any more than successful hangmen (another regrettable necessity for the protection of society, we were told) did. The war dead would have no more claim to public memorials than have women dying in childbirth or workers killed in industrial accidents. The Heir to the Throne would not see fit to get married in naval uniform, his hand on a sword. Military Tattoos, Beating the Retreat, the Royal Tournament, Trooping the Colour and Open Days at military bases would have all the appeal of day-trips round a morgue or sewage works, and Little Soldier Kits would be recognised as ranking in tastefulness with Little Yorkshire Ripper Outfits. There would be no such song as Onward Christian Soldiers, our national anthem would not mention victory, and Army Chaplain would be as meaningful a job-title as Vegetarian Butcher. Remembrance Day – supposedly a day for grief over the pain and wastage of war – would be just that, and the politicians would lay their wreaths last, not first, behind the war-disabled, widowed, orphaned, not ahead of them, recognising, as politicians, that war is their failure and nobody's triumph. And there would be fairies at the bottom of all gardens. The war movement celebrates war at every opportunity, and we do not celebrate what we only regard as a regrettable necessity, let alone what we hate.

The peace movement celebrates life. The Greenham Common women's peace camp began with a group of women walking to the planned cruise missile base to protest about the threat it represented to life on earth. And they didn't go home. They brought caravans and tents, they bent saplings and covered them with tarpaulins and plastic, and lived there. Arrested, evicted, shot at, robbed, threatened, criticised, insulted, soaked and chilled on some occasions; idolised, supported, imitated, sun-warmed, welcomed, prayed for, immortalised, loved and willed to success on others, they've been there two years and at the time of writing (September 1983) are there still. As women they call patriarchy's bluff. A woman's place is in the home, women are the nurturers of life. And so the women of Greenham Common make homes and nurture life right there, a few feet away from men preparing to destroy both. You women are so emotional. You take everything so personally. Exactly.

The webs of wool in the woods, round the bases, the courts, the prisons, have many symbolic meanings. It helps to have read *Gyn/Ecology* by Mary Daly (Women's Press, 1979). From the looks of things, the policemen with the clipboards and wellies, puzzling over the tangled-up women in the mud, have not read it. (Cartoon question marks hovering over their heads would not look out of place.) Mary Daly traces the original meaning of Spinster – not, as now, a woman defined by the fact that she has not been had by a husband, but a woman with an honourable and marketable skill and consequently no need of a husband: a woman whose occupation is to spin.

And spinning is symbolic too of a way of thinking that confronts, subverts and turns away from the deadly ejaculatory intellectualising of the war movement, symbolised so neatly in its own creation, the cruise missile (wasn't a cruise once something peaceful?), one of whose features is that once taken from its silo and launched (wasn't a silo once a place where food was stored for cattle?) it cannot be recalled. 'Spinsters spin and weave,' says Mary Daly, 'mend-ing and creating unity of consciousness . . . spinsters span the dichotomies of false consciousness and break its mindbinding combinations.'

Spinning and weaving and striving to see things in their wholeness, the peace movement refuses to accept the war movement's assessment of itself, to allow it to have all the answers for the simple reason that it devised all the questions. (Which would you rather be, red or dead? If the other side have got them, haven't we got to have them too?) The peace movement asks questions of its own, questions which, whether they come from feminism, pacifism, moralism, alternative versions of strategic studies or gutwringing terror, share a common refusal to think in militaristic straight lines.

Who exactly are 'we' and who are the 'other side' and who says so? However the different national tendencies within the international war movement line up for the next – last – world war, it will really be soldiers and politicians versus civilians. This is not to say that millions of low-grade soldiers and politicians won't die, but as a group they'll be better equipped to survive than the rest of us, and their masters will be in shelters along with national art treasures. The dictionary defines 'civilian' by exclusion – 'person not in the army, navy or air force' – as if we were a minority. But that's the 'we' I belong to.

Why are some nuclear powers identified as friends and others as foes when all by definition have indicated their willingness to destroy the earth or as much of it as they can manage? In what sense is a limited nuclear war limited and what precisely are its advantages for those of us who live within its limits, as the UK, aircraft-carrier to the United States, undoubtedly will be?

Why do we have to be red or dead? Is it not possible to be neither? Or both?

Even if we were to accept that owning nuclear

weapons defended us from the risk of enemy attack, why are we supposed to see defence against *that* risk as more important than the defence a properly funded health service might provide against other premature deaths, or better roads against road accidents, or industrial investment against the destitution and disorder that come from unemployment? How have we come to see nuclear weapons as more life-preserving than food?

Henry Kissinger himself – who is no spinster – asked: 'What in the name of God is strategic superiority? What do you do with it?' To put it another way – if we already have enough nuclear firepower to kill the earth and everything on it, why do we need anything else?

If arming yourself to the teeth prevents you from being attacked, why are British women prosecuted for carrying knives to protect themselves from male assault on the streets? Why – and this is what it comes down to – why is the human male so aggressive and dangerous, so ingeniously destructive?

A woman's banner once said: 'The hand that changed the nappy will never press the button.' Well, let's hope not, for the finger on Britain's button almost certainly changed Mark's and Carol's nappies, or at least supervised the nanny. It is not necessary to declare Margaret Thatcher a (dis)honorary male in order to identify the war movement as a predominantly male phenomenon; all she proves is that women are allowed to join, and we knew that anyway. Similarly, it is not necessary to pretend that the peace movement is composed entirely of women to recognise that it is those qualities traditionally attributed to women (whether by nature or nurture we don't know, but let's hope it's nurture because if men can't learn them, they're doomed, or we all are) that will save us: nurturance, nonviolence, a distrust of abstract theories and a preference instead for taking things personally and getting a bit emotional about them. Things like genocide.

This 'taking it personally' style of protest may be new – I say *may be* because if the study of women's and other oppressed groups' history has taught us anything, it is that very little is new; it is part of the oppression to bury the history – but the demand of women, men and children for freedom from the nuclear threat is not. It's important that we remember this while struggling for more effective ways of making that demand. 'New' is a mixed blessing of a word. Newspapers love it – what is not new, is not news – and a nonviolent mass movement relies on moral force and public opinion, reachable chiefly through mass media. But 'new' dishonours those who have gone before (ironically, even the radical press hailed Joan Ruddock as the 'first woman' to chair CND, erasing April Carter, Sheila Oakes and Olive Gibbs at a stroke) and prevents us learning from our past. So I'd like to end on this personal note.

I first joined CND in 1962. I'd seen a demonstration in which a child in a push chair carried a placard with the words: 'I want to die of old age.' A fit, privileged teenager of the welfare state, I had taken it for granted that I would die of old age, if at all. Death was not even on my horizon. The words on that child's banner (I wonder if she remembers?) meant that it was. It was the era of Mutually Assured Destruction, the strategy that said that since the USA and the USSR could blow each other sky high any time they liked, neither would, and so we were all safe. There were of course a few jarring notes in this cosy world view (and cosy is not too cosy a word for its stability, viewed backwards from an era when limited nuclear wars, winnable nuclear wars and first strikes are affably discussed) – the odd near-miss, and an atmospheric nuclear testing programme laying down slow-action carcinogens in the bones of all of us, not to mention the nightmare image of the four-minute warning. (We now know we cannot even rely on four minutes. It may be even longer.) These, together with the moral horror of it all, brought us out on to the streets in our tens of thousands.

And then what happened? The 1963 Test Ban Treaty seemed like a victory – few of us appreciated that the superpowers didn't need to test in the atmosphere any longer anyway, they could carry on underground. The 1964 Labour election victory seemed like a victory . . . but in the disillusion that followed, the issue seemed to go away. Vietnam, women's liberation, racial conflict, students' rights, not to mention my own personal life and career, all seemed more important. An almost total media blackout on discussion of 'the bomb' helped. I lived in Scotland for a while, and well remember a Scottish student, in 1971, making indignant mention of the US missiles at Holy Loch, the Polaris submarines at Faslane. 'Are they still there, then?' I said in surprise.

Where did I think they'd gone?

In 1973-4 I worked on the staff of CND – a CND that had to spell out its name in full if you wanted people to know who you were talking about, and thought it was doing well if it got twenty people on a picket, and was referred to in the press (if at all) in the past tense. But the realisation that the mass withdrawal of support from the campaign since the early Sixties had been matched only by the steady build-up of arms, unchecked by SALT treaties or detente, overwhelmed me again, and once again I joined the ranks of those thousands who 'used to be in CND' but now preferred to tackle more tangible issues, since there was obviously nothing to be done about the arms race.

The peace movement of the early 1980s – renewed but not new – says, it is intolerable that we do nothing. I am writing this in the autumn of 1983, a grey, chilly time after a warm summer. Barring miracles, the boys of RAF/USAF Greenham Common will have their toys in time for Christmas: 96 Ground-Launched Cruise Missiles, each of them capable of repeating the Hiroshima atrocity ten times over.

Barring miracles. The peace movement is visible, vociferous and growing. Somewhere in the background, the US/USSR missile control negotiations mutter on. Occasionally the word 'breakthrough' leaks out into a headline, with the suggestion that perhaps Cruise won't be needed after all. And that's when my fear that the missiles will come is matched by the fear that they won't; that the war movement will negotiate them away (as it did with atmospheric nuclear testing) and get to work on something else. The peace movement will be allowed to think it has won a victory, and the arms race will continue unabated. It has happened before.

At the time of reading this, you will know which of these things has happened. Has another 'arms control' trick been played? Or are the missiles there at Greenham, safe behind the decorated wire, deep in their danced-upon silos? I will not ask – has the peace movement routed the war movement, served it notice to quit Greenham, and Molesworth and Upper Heyford, Aldermaston and Westminster and the Clyde . . . that will take longer than the production time of this book. But the 1980s peace movement will not be destroyed by setbacks or sent home by war movement deceptions, for the simple reason that it is already at home: literally and figuratively it has made its home on the war movement's doorstep, and it may be evicted but it will not be moved.

Peace camps and direct action

31 Woman from Greenham Common Peace Camp, Westminster, January 1982

32 Greenham Common October 1981, several weeks after the Camp was first established

33 Picket, missile silo construction site, Greenham Common, February 1982

34 Missile silo construction site, Greenham Common, March 1982

35 Spring Festival, Greenham Common, March 1982

36 24-Hour Blockade after the Spring Festival, Greenham Common, March 1982. Some women were arrested for obstructing the highway and found guilty. Those refusing to pay fines were sent to prison for seven days

37 Protest against the arrest of demonstrators picketing the hearing for an eviction order on the Greenham Common Women's Peace Camp, High Court, London, May 1982

38 Arrest of demonstrator, High Court, May 1982

39 Stop the City, Bank of England, September 1983

40 Die-in, Stock Exchange, June 1982

41 Die-in, City of London, June 1982

42-5 Occupation of security-box, Main Gate, Greenham Common, August 1982. Eighteen women were charged with breach of the peace and found guilty. Those who refused to be bound over were sent to prison for 14 days.

46 Outside Main Gate, Greenham Common, March 1983

47 Outside Main Gate, Aldermaston, April 1983

48 USAF/RAF Upper Heyford, Oxfordshire, June 1983

49 Main Gate, Greenham Common, March 1983

1 Brambles Farm Peace Camp, Waterlooville, Hants, May 1982. Set up following the lead given by Greenham Common; others include those at Bradenham Estate, Bridgend, Burghfield, Burtonwood, Caerwent, Capenhurst, Daws Hill, Fairford, Faslane, Hexham, Lakenheath, Lossiemouth, Molesworth, Nap Hill, Upper Heyford and Waddington

30 Boulders dumped by Newbury Council on the site of Greenham Common Women's Peace Camp, after eviction by the Department of Transport, October 1982. 'The Council could not have provided us with a better visual aid as to what Berkshire will look like after the Bomb' (Greenham Woman). The Peace Camp moved nearby

52-5 Obstruction of building work, Main Gate, Greenham Common, October 1982. The large webs were a symbolic protection to the land. Thirteen women were charged with breach of the peace and found guilty. Those who refused to be bound over were sent to prison for 14 days

54

56-8 Embrace the Base, Greenham Common, December 1982. 30,000 women linked arms around the base and decorated the fence

59-61 Close the Base, Greenham Common, December 1982. 2,000 women took part in a blockade

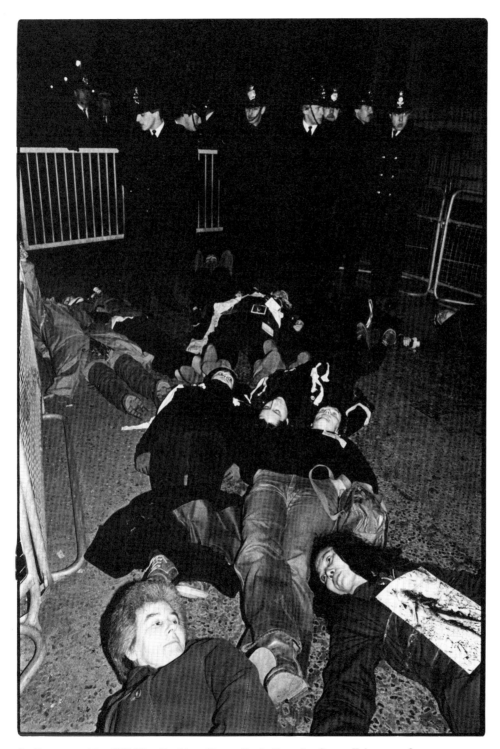

62 Protest at visit of US Vice-President George Bush, Downing Street, February 1983

63 Arrest, blockade of Upper Heyford, June 1983. 752 people were arrested during the five–day blockade

64 Arms are for linking, International Women's Blockade, Greenham Common, July 1983. A five-day blockade

65 Day of Action, Upper Heyford, December 1982. 1,000 people took pa

PROHIBITED PLACE
PHOTOGRAPHING AND
SKETCHING FORBIDDEN

66 Blockade, Royal Ordnance Factory, Burghfield, March 1983